Peter

Written by Ian Kitchen
Design by Catherine Jackson
Cover design by Wild Associates

Copyright ©1999 CPAS

Church Pastoral Aid Society
Athena Drive
Tachbrook Park
WARWICK
CV34 6NG
Tel: (01926) 458458

ISBN 1 902041 04 6

No unauthorized copying. Permission is given to copy the 'Group Sheet' handouts for groups whose leader is using this book.

Scripture quotations taken from the HOLY BIBLE, NEW INTERNATIONAL VERSION, copyright © 1973, 1978, 1984 by International Bible Society. Used by permission.

Church Pastoral Aid Society
Registered Charity no 1007820
A company limited by guarantee
CPAS

Think it Out – Act it Out!

What's Christianity all about? Salvation? Living in a way which glorifies God? Reflecting Jesus in our lives? God in action, claiming a people for himself? Well, yes, all these and more. And the great news is that all these topics are found in the two short letters of 1 and 2 Peter. What we have here is really a wonderful summary, dating from very early in Christian history, of what Christians believe and how they need to live as a result.

In both letters, Christians are urged to think through and live out their faith in the context of a surrounding culture which does not understand them and is frequently hostile to them. The suffering about which 1 Peter constantly speaks almost certainly comes in an informal way from this surrounding culture rather than from organized 'official' persecution. And in 2 Peter pagan teaching and behaviour are seen to be weaselling their way into the Church itself. These are relevant letters for us today!

Both letters focus on the hope which Christians have of Jesus' return at the end of time to judge the world and to complete the rescue of his people which is assured by his death and resurrection. So there is plenty of space devoted to the second coming and to persevering until that happens. We'll be exploring the implications of that for us today, as well.

These letters aren't given to us just to increase our knowledge (although they will do that). Over and over they lead us on from understanding to asking, 'Well, then, what do we need to do about this?' We'll try to find some answers to those questions as we work through the material, as well as suggesting some avenues for churches to explore for themselves. Peter's letters are practical, and we hope that you'll find this resource practical too.

Question of attribution?

It must be said that many people think Peter the apostle didn't write both letters – the second one in particular is thought doubtful. Don't let that cloud your study of them. Even if Peter was not the author (and he may well have been), their purpose is clear. The writer or writers come from a background strongly connected with Peter and they state and defend true apostolic teaching, protecting the Church against hardship, doubts and false teaching. There is no intention to confuse or mislead anyone: the form and contents would have pointed early readers to the true position. What is said in both letters would have met with warm approval from Peter himself, and so the Church accepted these writings into the Bible. For the same reason, and for convenience, we refer to the author as 'Peter' throughout this book.

Contents

HOW DO I USE THIS BOOK?		page 4
HOW DO I PREPARE?		page 5

1 HOPE-FOCUSED — page 6
1 Peter 1
AIM To see the greatness of what God has promised to give Christians

2 SOMEBODY UP THERE LIKES ME — page 10
1 Peter 2
AIM To explore some of the richness and challenge of what Jesus has done for us

3 SKIN-DEEP? — page 14
1 Peter 3
AIM To place our relationships on a godly basis

4 TWO WAYS TO LIVE — page 18
1 Peter 4
AIM To assess ourselves in the light of God's coming judgement

5 BECAUSE... BECAUSE... — page 22
1 Peter 5
AIM To have humility for the present and outrageous ambitions for the future

6 GETTING IT STRAIGHT — page 26
2 Peter 1
AIM To appreciate that our faith is securely based, but never static

7 DANGER AHEAD! — page 30
2 Peter 2
AIM To be aware of the dangers posed by false teaching, and to be ready to confront them

8 FUTURE PERFECT! — page 34
2 Peter 3
AIM To sum up Peter's message and to set a course for the future

BECAUSE OF HIM... — page 38
Mime activity based on 1 Peter 2:21-25

SILENT DISCUSSION — page 39
Activity based on 1 Peter 5

DEFEND THE FAITH — page 40
Discussion activity based on 2 Peter 2

How do I Use this Book?

Project Peter is a series of eight studies. Each is a complete unit, but they also follow on from one another. Each study contains the sections listed below.

ON THE FIRST TWO PAGES

AIM The intended outcome of the study.

INTRODUCTION Some general points about the topic and its teaching content.

NOTES Some comments on the passages that will help you as you prepare. You may want to read some of these to the group if you think they would be helpful. But be sparing with them, because they are meant chiefly for your benefit as you prepare.

YOUNG FOCUS Some ideas for introducing children's and youth groups to the passage. We hope that much of the main study material could be adapted for other age groups as well, and some adult groups will find these Young Focus ideas fun and helpful – try some out! Alert your youth and children's leaders to the existence of these ideas.

THE NEXT PAGE IS THE...

GROUP SHEET This may be photocopied. *(Please see details in the copyright note on page 1.)* It has all the basic material for a Bible study on the week's passage, and contains:

WAY IN An activity or discussion starter to help people to begin to think about the topic and share their own experiences where appropriate. We have provided a variety of activities: be adventurous if some of them are new to your group!

BIBLE STUDY Questions to help the group explore the teaching of the passage.

The **Looking at the text** section ensures that everyone has a basic grasp of the text. **Applying the text** links the themes of the passage with our own lives today.

ACTION Suggested steps for the group, or your church fellowship as a whole, to take for a practical working out of what has been learned.

ON THE OPPOSITE PAGE FOR EASY REFERENCE THERE ARE...

ADDITIONAL QUESTIONS These dig deeper into the text and expand the scope of the discussion. You can integrate some of them with questions on the **GROUP SHEET**, or you can work through them separately.

LEARNING ACTIVITIES These are designed to help groups get a different angle on the passage and the issues that it raises.

WORSHIP AND PRAYER Suggestions for things to do at the group meeting or during Sunday worship. We have assumed that groups which want to sing will find their own appropriate songs, and have concentrated on ideas for helping people respond to God's word without music.

How do I Prepare?

1 PREPARE YOURSELF

Pray about the passage, the study, the group and yourself as leader.

Read through the passage carefully. The notes and questions in *Project Peter* are based on the New International Version of the Bible.

Work quickly through the **GROUP SHEET** as if you were an ordinary group member. Jot down notes, questions and areas to expand or work on. Be honest with yourself and let God teach you as you prepare.

Read through the passage again and check the **NOTES**. Be guided by the **AIM** and **INTRODUCTION**.

2 PLAN YOUR APPROACH

Decide how you are going to tackle the study. There are a number of possible approaches to each passage, depending on which questions and activities you use. You may decide to take more than one meeting over a study in order to make use of all the material.

Some groups will benefit if all the members read the passage through beforehand, in which case you'll need to remind people to do this. Others will prefer to come to it fresh and be guided completely by the group leader.

You can use the material on the **GROUP SHEET** every week, and you can also use the **ADDITIONAL QUESTIONS** to substitute for or supplement the questions on the **GROUP SHEET**. We recommend that you always include **WAY IN** and **ACTION**.

Because the **WORSHIP AND PRAYER** section does not contain suggestions for songs, you'll need to think about what to sing, if your group wants to include this in its meetings.

3 ASSESS THE TIMING

You will not have time to cover all the material, so don't set out thinking that this is the aim. No one will be deducting marks if the paper is not completed! You need to use what is appropriate and helpful to your group – you need not even cover the whole passage, although the sessions aim to help you do so. Think carefully about the timing of each section. We have not put down suggestions for times, since each group will have different priorities. However, we suggest that as you prepare you should write down your target time for each section.

Try to keep to a basic framework each week and allocate times for prayer, reading, discussion and refreshments; however, you may feel that a longer prayer time, for example, is appropriate on some occasions. It is important to begin and end promptly so that those who need to go can do so without embarrassment, leaving others to chat if they wish.

Hope-focused

1 PETER 1

AIM

To see the greatness of what God has promised to give to Christians

INTRODUCTION

How encouraging for these scattered and suffering Christians in what is now Turkey to receive this letter, in which the great apostle writes so reassuringly to them. In this first chapter his message comes across loud and clear – no matter what the opposition, we belong to God. This doesn't mean that we're cosseted or will always feel close to God, but we are protected in that we are assured of our ultimate end and are given grace now to endure. Verses 1 and 2 remind us that we may not be well known to the world or even to each other, but God knows us perfectly and marks us out as his.

Grace is a constant theme of this letter (1:2,10,13 and other examples later). It refers to God's decision to bless and save us even though we don't deserve that he should.

NOTES

1:2 There is relatively little in this letter about the Holy Spirit, but he's there in the background of Peter's thinking and here we have a good run-down of the work of the different persons within the Trinity. 'Sprinkling' with Jesus' blood is a picture from Old Testament sacrifices.

1:3-4 What a good summary of the benefits of Christianity – and good verses to meditate on for a few minutes in your preparation. 'New birth' (see also 1:23) is a way of saying that we become completely new people when we turn to God. The rest of this letter shows that, just as being born physically is only a start to the rest of our life, so being born again spiritually requires us to live in a particular way from then on.

1:5 The idea of things (and particularly Jesus) being 'revealed' is characteristic of this letter – look out for further examples of God communicating to us about himself.

1:6 The suffering Peter talks about throughout the letter is persecution and suffering because of Jesus, rather than illness and so on, even though we might refer to these as 'trials'.

1:7 Faith is worth far more than material things (compare 1:18). To build our faith, God will use hard times for our ultimate good.

1:10-12 The Old Testament points to Jesus. Those who wrote it down did not know exactly what they were leading up to, but for us who know Jesus it is important in building up our understanding of him. And if 'angels long to look into these things' then they must be precious.

1:13 As always for Peter, knowledge leads to action in practical, everyday terms. Note that the focus is on our future hope, not the present time, which can never be as good and may be frankly horrible, even for Christians.

1:15-16 This quote from Leviticus 11:44-45 means that people should be able to say of Christians 'like Father, like child,' seeing his purity (holiness) clearly reflected in us.

1:17 The knowledge that we will all be judged by God should lead to a different way of life, rejecting the world's values and its fleeting rewards. It's all part of taking our Father's character seriously, not trying to work our way to heaven (because we cannot) but building a true relationship with him.

1:18 Reference to the 'empty way of life' shows that most of Peter's readers were Gentiles rather than Jews, whose forefathers were at least working along the right lines.

1:19 'Blood' is a key Old Testament word standing for 'life'. The reference here is to the system of sacrifices, and stresses that Jesus was the perfect sacrifice who gave himself to die in our place, once and for all.

1:20 This verse hints at the greatness and permanence of God's plan – and it's on our behalf!

1:21 We believe in God through Christ. Jesus is the only way to the Father, and to believe in Jesus is to believe in God and be saved (compare 1:8-9).

1:23-24 Here is our exciting destiny, given through God's grace. Peter stresses the enduring relevance and value of God's word, without which we would know none of this.

YOUNG FOCUS

Adapt the following starter ideas and questions according to the age of your children's or youth group, to give them a way into the passage.

Peter wishes his readers 'grace and peace'. Choose someone in the news and decide what you would wish them. Then make them a card, find the address and send it.

Make a shining, tin-foil diamond and write the great phrases from 1:3-5 on different facets of it. Pairs could prepare an explanation of a particular phrase for the rest of the group.

Make some shields from cardboard and let people try to protect themselves from flying table-tennis balls, jelly, eggs, bat dung or whatever you choose. Talk about what it means for God to 'shield' us.

Hide some pictures of things associated with Jesus: a cross, crown of thorns, a manger, fishermen with nets, and so on. Have a hunt for them, with prizes especially if those who find each picture can explain its connection with Jesus. Talk about how great it is that God revealed himself in Jesus, rather than leaving us to guess our way towards him. Lead into thinking about the further revelation of Jesus which we hear of at the end of 1:7.

Research some Old Testament prophecies of Jesus' coming. How many can the group find? How clearly do the prophecies speak of Jesus?

Pick a couple of big occasions that are coming up for group members and ask how they are going to prepare for them. Lead into 1:13 and the need to prepare for Jesus' return.

What is the most precious thing that group members possess? Get them to describe it without naming it, while the rest of the group guess what it is. Then discuss what is God's most precious possession, and look at 1:18-19.

Hope-focused

1 PETER 1

AIM
To see the greatness of what God has promised to give to Christians

WAY IN
Each group member should sum up himself or herself in no more than ten words and share that description with the group. Then look at 1:1-2, which defines what a Christian is.

BIBLE STUDY Read 1 Peter 1
Looking at the text
What insight into the roles within the Trinity do we get from 1:2? How does this fit in with how we usually think of the Father, Son and Spirit?

If you had to find a 'motto' in this chapter which summed up Christianity, what verse or verses would you choose?

What purposes can we identify in the 'trials' that Christians sometimes have to endure? (1:6-7)

What should we be looking for when we read the Old Testament? (1:10-11)

What should be the distinguishing features of Christians, according to this passage? (1:13-16)

What answer would you give to the question 'What is God like?', based on 1:17-25?

Applying the text
Verses 8 and 9 are a description of what Christians should be like, and a great challenge. What does it mean for us to 'love Jesus' (1:8) – in terms of our feelings, our behaviour and our attitudes?

Is 'an inexpressible and glorious joy' typical of us? If it's sometimes lacking, what does the passage suggest we need to meditate on more?

Peter's quotation from Leviticus (1:16) stresses that we should be holy, like our Father God. So should we all become monks or nuns? What does it mean for us in our daily lives and in the situations in which we tend to find ourselves?

What do 1:17,22 require of each of us, in practical terms, for the next week?

ACTION
Encourage your church leaders to reflect on 1:1 and the reality of suffering, both in this letter and in the Church today. Ask for volunteers to send messages of love and support to churches abroad, especially in places where people are suffering for being Christians. You can get suggestions from Christian Solidarity Worldwide, PO Box 99, New Malden, Surrey KT3 3YF, Tel: (0181) 942 8810. Make sure that any replies are shared with the congregation; perhaps a lasting relationship can be built up.

ADDITIONAL QUESTIONS

1. Bad things still happen to Christians, and often the best people seem to suffer most. So what does it mean to say that we are 'shielded by God's power' (1:5)?

2. In the light of 1:13, what possible rivals are there in our lives to the hope that is focused on the future?

3. How would you try to convince a sceptical neighbour that Jesus' sacrifice is more valuable than silver or gold?

LEARNING ACTIVITIES

1. Wish list
Everyone should think of three things they are hoping for in the next year and give each a rating between 1 (lowest) and 10 (highest) according to how important these things are to them. Share just a few, if people are happy to do so. Then ask them to give a similar rating to the thought of dying in the next year. Any 10s? Talk this through in the light of 1:13. Jesus Christ being 'revealed' is a reference to his second coming.

2. Going, going, gone
Have a mock 'auction' of items based on people in the news: a famous footballer's skills, an Oscar-winner's acting ability, a celebrity broadcaster's charisma – and so on. How much would people give for each? Then look at 1:18-19. God paid the most incredibly high price – for us! A brief time of thanks may be appropriate at this point.

3. The real thing
Give the group a stack of newspapers and magazines. Ask them to tear out advertisements reflecting qualities which are valued in the world. Discuss whether God could or would appear in any of these ads. What essentials would have to go into an advertisement describing God? What does 1:15-16 have to say on these questions, and what does 'holiness' mean for us in practical terms?

WORSHIP AND PRAYER

The main part of the letter starts, in 1:3, with praise. That's a good place for us to start as well – praising God for what he's done for us and for what lies in store in the future. You could fill a big sheet of paper with items for which to thank him.

Then you could think, in the light of 1:18-19, of ways in which we can worship God through our giving.

Verse 16 can lead us to worship God through making our lives more holy: read together Psalm 15 and have a time to meditate on it. People may appreciate some 'private time' to think about or write down areas of struggle and then pray about them.

Living in love within our fellowship is also part of our worship. Use 1:22 as an encouragement to share the peace together and heal any differences within the group. Then finish with praise again, in prayer or song, putting the focus firmly back on God as you finish this session.

2

Somebody Up There Likes Me

1 PETER 2

AIM
To explore some of the richness and challenge of what Jesus has done for us

INTRODUCTION
Peter here deals with living within the church and within different areas of society. Every question about why we should act in a particular way basically receives the answer, 'Because of Jesus'. From that basis Peter's vision focuses in to look at Jesus' death, and at how that acts as a model for Christians when they have to make decisions about how to behave. But that's not the only effect of Jesus' death: we're reminded of God's grace in taking away our sin, and so we are left humble again.

NOTES

2:1 As so often in this letter, Peter calls for a practical response to what he has said – here, in taking action against vices that can destroy a community, which is what the Church should be (see 2:5).

2:2 'Milk' here is not associated with immaturity (as elsewhere in the New Testament) but with healthy nourishment. We need to keep feeding on the word of God throughout our Christian lives.

2:3 The 'Lord' here echoes Psalm 34:8 and the word is used there about God. But it is also identified with the 'him' of 2:4 – Jesus is recognized here as God.

2:4-5 This identification of believers with Jesus is one of the most astonishing things about God's work on our behalf. It's a great motivation for us to take the right approach to life and to other people which Peter urges on us.

2:6 This is the first of several quotes by which Peter backs up his statement in 1:10, showing that the Old Testament foreshadowed Jesus. Verses 6 to 8 stress that everyone must encounter Jesus and make a response to him based on faith. In 2:8, note that a right response to God's message also includes obedience. As usual, Peter is seeking practical action.

2:9-12 Whereas Peter has elsewhere called for inward results to come from faith (1:13; 2:1,11), here he calls for outward action. A balanced Christian life should display both.

2:13-20 Faith should affect every aspect of life. It cannot be a private affair. Peter starts to dig into some of the toughest relationships – with the government and at work – where Christian principles may be most easily forgotten. Since many slaves worked in households, domestic relationships are also touched on here.

2:18 Legally speaking, slaves were not 'full persons', but Christianity treated them the same as free people. Compare Jesus' attitude towards society's outsiders (for example, Luke 5:27-32). There's another challenge to us. In Peter's world slavery was the lot of a high percentage of the population. It imposed set duties while giving shape to the bulk of daily life and so offering many temptations for the growth of resentment, cheating and so on. Similarities with the world of modern employment lie not far from the surface.

2:20-25 There are several hints in these verses of incidents in the passion which Peter would have witnessed. His urging to imitate Christ has painful personal recollection behind it, making it all the more compelling. Verse 25 holds echoes of his own denial of Jesus (John 18) and his subsequent restoration and commissioning (John 21).

YOUNG FOCUS

Adapt these starter ideas and questions according to the age of your children's or youth group, to give them a way into the passage.

Write the vices from 2:1 on separate slips of paper. Make sure everyone knows what they all mean, think about how they might sneak into our lives, and then screw them up or get rid of them in some other way. You could go on to do the same with things from the past week which group members wish they had not done.

Get a load of sweets, biscuits etc. Find a long song about God being good to us (or sing a short one several times), stopping to eat something after each verse. Taste how good he is, and remember – God doesn't rot your teeth.

Invite group members to bring (with permission) items of jewellery. Together, see what you can build from them. Photograph any good results. It's pretty difficult, but 2:7 tells us that God builds with precious stones (and see Revelation 21:19-21).

Label one end of the room 'heads' and the other 'tails'. Tell group members that you are going to flip a coin – but before you do so, they must predict the outcome by going to the end of the room of their choice. Flip the coin after they have moved. Everyone at the 'wrong' end of the room is eliminated. Now ask those still 'in' to predict the outcome of your second flip of the coin. Carry on until everyone is out. Now discuss the fact that there are two possible destinations for people (2:7-8). How do we make sure of going to the right one?

Make some tin-foil crowns, haloes and rings and get some torches. Equip the group (royal, holy and married to God) for a procession with some praise thrown in. Make sure they know why Christians have been so honoured – the end of 2:9 tells them.

Talk about times when something unfair has happened to group members. Discuss how they felt. Then talk about times when they have done something they don't like in order to help others. Are they prepared to do these things on a regular basis in order to honour God? Verses 19 and 20 imply that they should be prepare to if circumstances require it. Now talk about a time when someone put them into a good position which they didn't deserve. God constantly does this for us.

Get some sheep impersonations going. Once everyone's convincing, send them off in different directions. At an arranged signal, they have to race back to a leader or an agreed place. That's what life is like (2:25).

Somebody Up There Likes Me

1 PETER 2

GROUP SHEET

AIM
To explore some of the richness and challenge of what Jesus has done for us

WAY IN
If your group is fit enough, carry one of the members around the room, first as a burden and then as a hero or heroine being chaired aloft. Otherwise, choose some suitable object and have someone carry it first as if it were a great burden and then holding it up like a trophy being shown off. Then look together at 2:24, and then at 2:9. Here are two sides of the same coin, showing something of what God has done for us.

BIBLE STUDY Read 1 Peter 2
Looking at the text
The vices mentioned in 2:1 may not seem to us like the most 'major' sins. Why do you think that Peter focuses on them here?

What does God want to achieve through the lives of Christians? (2:4-12)

Christians are, apparently, human beings. In what way are they 'aliens and strangers in the world'? (2:11)

Try to summarize the principles laid down in 2:18-20 – in a single sentence! How does this match up with how Jesus acted towards the end of his life?

Peter gives more than one reason why Jesus died on the cross. What are these reasons?

Applying the text
What signs of growth can you identify in yourself (2:2) over, say, the past six months?

How effective are we at declaring God's praises (2:9)? What more might we do?

What limits do we set to the instruction given in 2:13 about submitting to authority? Should we set any limits at all?

What different kinds of people are we in regular contact with, and what is a proper way to show respect to each?

How do Peter's instructions to slaves apply to our relationships at work today?

Verse 21 says that Christians are called to bear up under unjust suffering if it comes. Should we be concerned if we never seem to experience such suffering?

ACTION
Read 2:12 alongside Matthew 5:16. How can we live so that those around us will be convinced of God's righteousness before they have to meet him on judgement day? As a group, or as a church, decide some concrete ways in which you can get involved in meeting social needs through 'good deeds', so as to witness to this effect.

ADDITIONAL QUESTIONS

1. Should it be easier to get relationships right with our fellow-believers (dealt with in the first few verses of the chapter) than with 'outsiders' (dealt with in the rest of it)? Does your answer reflect what we find in practice?

2. In the light of 2:4-5, have we ever thought of ourselves as identified so closely with Jesus? It's a great privilege, to which we should respond. What does it mean in practice to offer 'spiritual sacrifices' to God? (Romans 12:1 and Hebrews 13:15-16 hold some useful clues.)

3. Have there been times when we have suffered unjust treatment because of our faith or because of the values that go with it? Did we react as Jesus would have done (2:23)? If not, what can we learn from the experience?

LEARNING ACTIVITIES

1. Vice squad
Produce sketch lasting no longer than thirty seconds to illustrate each of the vices in 2:1 as they might operate in a church setting. It may be easiest to keep them light-hearted and exaggerated. Don't make them about personalities in your own fellowship, or you'll become part of the problem!

2. Rocky house
Having read 2:4-5, get some stones and try to build a structure with them. What are the problems and joys of the task?

3. Battle stations
Verse 11 shows that there is no neutrality in spiritual matters. Watch the D-Day scene at the opening of the film *Saving Private Ryan*, or a similar war scene, and discuss how this is relevant to the Christian life. (There is a danger of being side-tracked by the impact of the film and the issues it raises. It's up to you whether to follow these up, either now or later.)

WORSHIP AND PRAYER

Verses 7 and 8 make it essential that we pray for those we know who are currently disobeying God's message, that he will bring them to himself before it is too late for them. You may like to commit yourself as a group to regular prayer for a limited number of such people.

It may be helpful to pray against each item in 2:1. These are vices which easily sneak under our guard.

A very effective impetus for prayer can be provided by miming 2:21-25. You can find a suggestion for a mime routine on page 38. This should lead to praise, but should also include a time of confession for times when we have done wrong, have not endured, have not followed Jesus example. After confession, assure each other of God's forgiveness by reading 2:24 to one another, loudly and with eye contact! You could consider offering to repeat your mime at a suitable point in a church service.

Use verses 9 and 10 as a basis for praise, focusing in turn on each description of what God has done for us. This could be very active – use lots of lights; dispel the darkness in a room or outside; have a festival or party. Sparklers, indoor fireworks and candles can all reinforce your praises.

Skin-deep?

1 PETER 3

AIM
To place our relationships on a godly basis

INTRODUCTION
This is not an easy chapter, but it is very rewarding – so please stick with it! It contains some introductory (and far from exhaustive) instructions on relationships between husbands and wives. Peter then moves from this to look at how we live with regard to others in the fellowship. Next he goes on to a topic which by now is becoming familiar: how to live right in suffering. Perhaps inevitably, this leads him to talk more about the work of Jesus. And good stuff it is, too.

NOTES

3:1-2 Wives are told to be as submissive as Jesus was, and for the same reason: to save souls. Peter points out that actions speak louder than words.

3:4 Compare this gentleness with 2:23. Peter is urging these wives to imitate Christ. He urged both men and women to do this earlier (2:21).

3:5-6 We may not place much emphasis on living up to the example of figures from history, but we shouldn't dismiss them too easily. Sarah and Abraham had a crucial part to play in God's plan of salvation. We may feel uncomfortable with Sarah calling Abraham 'master'. In her day it may not have implied as much submissiveness as we assume, but Peter certainly sees that aspect as significant.

3:7 Husbands are to act 'in the same way' – Peter does not see anything different in principle between how husbands and wives should behave, though he makes the point that wives are physically weaker and more vulnerable.

3:8-12 These verses can be seen as summing up Peter's ethical teaching. The theme of 'holiness' which we looked at in chapter 1 would be a good one-word label for their content. The quotation is from Psalm 34. Peter used that Psalm in 2:3 as well: it would be worth reading with the group.

3:13-14 No one should have any reasonable grounds to attack Christians who live as Peter instructs, but some will still suffer. Jesus promised this too (Matthew 5:10; 10:28). He also promised the greatest possible rewards to those who endure – see Revelation 2:7 and the endings to the other letters in Revelation 2 and 3.

3:15 The first sentence of this verse speaks of an absolute commitment to Jesus. Compare it with Isaiah 8:13. As elsewhere in this letter, what the Old Testament tells us is due to God can now be seen to be rightfully Christ's.

3:18 Here is one of Peter's great summaries of why Jesus died. Note that he died 'once for all' – there is no need for anything else to put us right with God.

3:19 Other uses of the Greek word in the Bible suggest that the 'spirits' in prison are rebellious spiritual beings rather than dead people. This ties in with Genesis 6:1-4. 'Preached' should then be understood as a proclamation of judgement against these spirits, based on Christ's victory over death, not as a call to repentance.

3:20 Noah and his family were a few people saved through water despite persecution. Peter uses this parallel for the small, persecuted churches of his day, who were distinctive because of their baptism with water.

3:21-22 The resurrection was God's way of confirming that Jesus' death was in line with his plan and was effective. Together with the ascension, the resurrection showed that Jesus had God's 'seal of approval'.

YOUNG FOCUS

Adapt these starter ideas and questions according to the age of your children's or youth group, to give them a way into the passage.

Bring in some old magazines *(Hello!/OK!)* and ask members to pick out pictures which are intended to show beautiful people (female and male). Discuss some times in real life, soaps, films or stories when good appearances have been deceptive. Look at Luke 11:33-36. It's the inside that counts.

Talk about times when people need to be submissive, and times when members have been considerate to others. How do we find a balance?

Read the first phrase of 3:8. Get everyone at once to sing a single note of their choice – the result should be pretty horrible. Allow people to breathe, but get them to continue on their notes until you touch them on the shoulder, one by one. Those you touch have to change to whatever note you're on (oh, yes, you don't get out of this one). Eventually you'll all be roughly in harmony (or unison, for the pedants among us). Doing it with our lives isn't so easy – what makes it hard?

Make a list of what makes us like someone. Check it against 3:8-9. Do we want to be like that? God wants us to. Do we care enough for him to live this way?

Prepare a parcel with many layers and a card with the words 'Jesus is Lord' buried right in the heart of it. Play pass the parcel until the message is reached. Discuss what it means to 'set apart Christ as Lord' in our hearts.

Practice for 3:15-16. Get members to answer the question, 'What's good about God?' Think of people with whom they may be able to share that simple message in the week ahead. Pray for the chance to do so.

Draw the scene mentioned in 3:22, and talk about how good it will be to be part of that scene.

And before we leave the subject of relationships, CPAS has a whole workbook of Bible-based teaching and activity on this theme. It's called *Me, You, Us, Them* and is aimed at the 11-18 age group. Want to know more? Call CPAS Sales on (01926) 458400.

GROUP SHEET

Skin-deep?

1 PETER 3

AIM
To place our relationships on a godly basis

WAY IN
Spend a minute or two reflecting on how you would like people to treat you. If you like, you could sketch out 'My Charter', headed 'In their dealings with me, people will...'. Share your ideas among the group and then look together at 3:8-9. Are we wishing for ourselves what God wants for us – or more, or less? (You may also like to think about whether you always treat other people in the way you want to be treated – see Matthew 7:12.)

BIBLE STUDY Read 1 Peter 3
Looking at the text
'In the same way' in 3:1,7 refers to what was said in 2:13, about paying proper respect to all because doing so pleases God. How does this principle of respect apply within marriage?

What general principles can you see here about wives? Should they also apply to husbands?

What fear might Peter be talking about in 3:6?

In what ways can our 'everyday' relationships affect our spiritual ones? (3:4,7)

According to 3:9,14, how should we react when people turn against us, and why?

In 3:21-22, is Peter saying that we are saved by baptism itself, or by what it symbolizes?

Applying the text
Read 3:3. What other outward things may we be tempted to show off or put our trust in?

Verse 4 recommends that we show a 'gentle and quiet spirit'. How can we cultivate such a spirit? Is it compatible with the 'inexpressible and glorious joy' of 1:8?

Share a little about people you know who embody the qualities described in 3:8-11. Is it realistic for us to try to achieve the kind of life described there?

With reference to 3:15-16, what approaches to evangelism have you come across which might actually put people off the gospel? How can we help each other to develop more 'gentleness and respect' In sharing our faith?

ACTION
As a group or a church, practise telling people about the gospel, and plan opportunities to share your faith. Many churches have found CPAS's *Lost for Words* course is very helpful for people who are not used to doing this. For further information contact CPAS by telephoning (01926) 458458.

ADDITIONAL QUESTIONS

1. Verse 1 talks of non-spoken witness, and 3:15-16 of spoken witness. Which are you better at? How can you use this strength, and how might you work to improve your weaker side?

2. In the light of 3:1-2,7, how do our own close relationships currently affect our spiritual lives?

3. Look at 3:8-9 alongside Matthew 5:3-12 and Galatians 5:22-23. How far do they overlap, and is there anything here which is not implied in those passages?

LEARNING ACTIVITIES

1. Suits you
What would you most not want people to say about your appearance? Make the effort to look like that for one day. How does it feel? Remind yourself constantly that God looks on the heart, not the outside, and ask what lessons you can learn from the experience. What insights does it give into 3:3-5? (This activity is for both sexes!) And, obviously, this needs tactful handling as it may raise painful issues for anyone with a physical impairment or disability.

2. What's in it for me?
Discuss or watch together some clips from TV soaps or films which show what the characters are seeking from their relationships. In the light 3:1-7, what should we be seeking?

3. Actions speak louder
Have someone make up a piece of good news and then tell it to the group in a totally inappropriate way (that is, very sadly, angrily and so on). Then do the same with a piece of bad news – telling it very happily, perhaps. Share some true experiences of behaviour and words not matching up, and look at 3:15-16 in the light of this.

WORSHIP AND PRAYER

Use 3:10-12 as a meditation leading to confession. Remember that the motivation for such good behaviour must be our faith – good deeds on their own don't impress the perfectly holy God.

Use 3:18 to reflect on how Jesus brought you to God. What other parts of the process can you think of? This might include people who told you the gospel, important events and so on. Share your stories with each other and give thanks to God for all these elements.

Verse 22 tells us something brilliant about Jesus. Take a large piece of paper and write 'Jesus' at the top. Underneath, write the names of any angels and saints you can think of, and some spiritual and human 'authorities and powers'. The latter may be good or bad. Pray prayers of praise to Jesus for his position above all these and for the fact that he is in control over them. It may be good also to pray for him to take action about some of the authorities and powers. If you must sing, how about 'Jesus shall take the highest honour'?

Two Ways to Live

1 PETER 4

AIM
To assess ourselves in the light of God's coming judgement

INTRODUCTION
This chapter brings together virtually all the themes we have some across earlier in the letter: love, suffering, godly living, God's tremendous grace to us, the coming return of Jesus, and the need to have right relationships within the church. However, this doesn't mean that Peter has run out of ideas and is just having to re-hash the same old stuff to fill up the space on his scroll. He's starting to turn some of the themes into more specific instructions to his readers, to keep their focus and motivation sharp. Perhaps the big question of the chapter is implied in 4:4 – which way are we going to go, God's or the ungodly world's?

NOTES

4:1 Another of the many 'therefores' in this letter (this time looking back to 3:18). Peter says that to look at Jesus will lead us to live in the right way. Conversely, if we want to live right, we need to look constantly at Jesus. To say that we are 'done with sin' if we have suffered is a difficult idea. It seems to carry the idea that if we enter into battle on God's behalf we will be better able to resist the temptation to evil acts – and, of course, in the longer term Christ's one-off act of suffering ensures our eventual freedom from sin's power.

4:5-6 Judgement is the big context for everyone's life, and is always in Peter's thinking (see 1:17 and 2:23). Verse 6 reminds us that even the dead will make a reappearance for the judgement – so Christians who have died will be vindicated. This was an important point for the early Christians, eagerly awaiting the second coming and a bit uncertain of the position of their fellow believers who had already died. People around might say that the deceased believers had been fooling themselves, but Peter stresses that God will restore them to life and so show that they were right in their faith and lifestyle.

4:8 The need for love underlies all the instructions for Christian living given in the next few verses (compare 1 Corinthians 13:1-3). The famous statement in 4:8b has been interpreted in a number of ways, but most likely means that love will enable us to overlook the sins of others against us – a vital thing within a persecuted community.

4:9 This verse originally concerned the reception given to travelling Christians ministering in an area for a short time, but we should think about how it applies to our time as well.

4:11 Peter focuses on gifts of service, perhaps remembering the episode recounted in John 13:12-17.

4:12 A new section in the chapter begins here, after the outburst of praise at the end of 4:11. There is a sense that Peter is starting to wind the letter up, recapping and filling in one or two gaps.

4:15 This may seem a rather odd list, and Peter's first readers might have thought the same – until they reached the last word. Being a busy-body and sticking our nose in where it's not needed is a great temptation for some, even within the church, and it causes a lot of trouble.

4:19 This makes a neat 'sandwich' of the chapter, picking up the similar thoughts of 4:1. The beginning and end of a piece of writing tend to be extra important, and Peter is driving his point home here.

YOUNG FOCUS

Adapt these starter ideas and questions according to the age of your children's or youth group, to give them a way into the passage.

Have a mock trial of a group member or leader for doing something extremely silly. If found guilty, have an equally silly punishment. Go on to talk about recent trials that have made the news. What sort of judge would members want if they were on trial? The whole of life should be seen in the perspective of judgement (4:5), and the prime characteristic of our judge is given in 2:23.

What would each member do if they had thirty minutes left to live? What final message would they leave to the world? What would they want for their last meal? Verse 7 calls for self-control in these circumstances, for a particular reason. Get members to pronounce on each other's normal ability to achieve self-control. Is the imminent end of the world motivation enough to try harder? Pray!

Read 4:10 and get people to identify what they are good at. It's usually helpful to get other people to make up for our own false modesty. How can we use each of the things identified to serve others?

Do the members tell their friends that they come to a Christian group, church and so on? What reactions do they get? Can we and they think of ways to support each other and make it easier to tell people?

Spend some time as a group building houses of playing cards. Without alerting the rest of the group, arrange for one person to be a 'meddler', joining in with over-helpful and clumsily destructive results. Before frustration levels reach boiling point, discuss how the activities of the 'plant' relate to 4:15.

Two Ways to Live

1 PETER 4

AIM
To assess ourselves in the light of God's coming judgement

WAY IN
Bring along a variety of fragrances – food, scented candles, oils and so on – and see if people can identify them 'blind'. You can do the same thing for taste, with different crisps, fruit pastilles or similar things. Perhaps include one or two nasty ones, if you're that sort of group. (The link of course, is with 4:4.)

BIBLE STUDY Read 1 Peter 4
Looking at the text
What might it mean to say that 'he who has suffered in his body is done with sin'?

Why do you think 4:7 gives prayer such a prominent place in the scheme of things (as does 3:7)?

In 4:8-11, why do you think that Peter has to urge his readers so strongly to do things which we might expect them to want to do? Is it their actions or their motivations which are mainly at fault?

How would you define the purpose of spiritual gifts? Is the emphasis in 4:10 a bit of a surprise?

Verses 13 and 14 say that it's a wonderful thing to be insulted and persecuted for Jesus. That sounds daft. What's so good about it?

Applying the text
Are there things less blatant than those listed in 4:3, which people are doing in our social circles and which we should take more care to keep away from?

Do we stand out as 4:4 clearly suggests that we should? What fragrance do we give off – that of the world, or the sweetness of Jesus? If you take the lid off a new jar of coffee, you can't avoid the fragrance. (Mmmm! Do it now!) Do people get the same unmissable distinctiveness from us?

What are the best ways to offer hospitality in your particular neighbourhood and with your particular fellow-Christians, friends and neighbours? Do we make the most of this very effective way of getting to know people?

ACTION
How do we show others that we bear the name of 'Christian'? If they don't know, they can't persecute us or join us! As a group or a church, plan some ways in which, individually and together, you can make it more obvious to others – possibly in ways which might intrigue them to find out more.

ADDITIONAL QUESTIONS

1. Do we really believe that 'The end of all things is near' (4:7)? How does the fact that Jesus might return at any moment affect our actions and our motivations?

2. What gifts are there in the group (4:10)? How can more opportunity be found to use them in their various forms? Make time to thank God for each gift identified – and remember that absolutely everyone has gifts.

3. Look at 4:15. How much danger is there of our falling into any of these categories? For most of us the big danger is 'meddler'. Share ways in which the danger may arise, and ways to avoid it.

LEARNING ACTIVITIES

1. Little angels

Put everyone's names into a hat, and each draw one out without saying whose it is. For the next week, everyone is the 'angel' of the person whose name they drew. They could leave them a little gift somewhere (set a financial limit), send them an encouraging card, or think of other things to do. And, of course, pray for them. But it must all be kept anonymous for now. Next week, reveal all! It's a small step on the road of 'loving each other deeply', but every little helps.

2. Service ace

Verse 10 says that gifts are for serving each other. Have a group meal and allocate everybody a servant role: cooking, decorating, hosting, dishing out the food, and so on. It might be the context for this meeting or for a separate Holy Communion, or just to have fun together, but be sure to include everyone as servants: there are no 'passengers' in this activity.

WORSHIP AND PRAYER

Make a list of all the things which are implied by 'The end of all things is near' – no more death, no more crying and so on. Thank God for all that is good on the list, and move on to further prayer. It would be good to provide everyone with a copy of the list so that they can use it to help follow the instructions of 4:7.

Follow up what was done as a result of the 'Action' section in session 1, particularly if letters were written and contacts made. At the least, pray about them, but perhaps it's time to take another practical step.

Thank God for the life and example of Christians who have died, but who we know will be vindicated at the great judgement when Jesus returns.

Copy onto slips of paper all the negative activities and descriptions found in this chapter – 'lust', 'thief' and so on. Read them through and pray that God will keep you from falling prey to any of them. Then burn them (mind that smoke alarm!) or tear them up. Write down and read aloud some activities and descriptions you want to be known by instead. Gather all these bits of paper together and pray about them, offering them to God as your intention for now and the future.

Because... Because...

1 PETER 5

AIM
To have humility for the present and outrageous ambitions for the future

INTRODUCTION
This chapter is much more than just a rounding off of the letter. As in other chapters, Peter moves from a particular example (church leaders) to general principles for all Christians. He repeats the need for humility and self-discipline and gives his final encouragement to endure suffering. Once again, this urging is based on the glory which awaits Christians at the end of time. That gives us the perfect closing note for this letter, whose whole purpose has been to encourage Peter's readers in godliness and perseverance because of the wonderful things which God has waiting for them.

NOTES

5:1 Peter avoids setting himself on a pedestal here. Unlike his hearers, he has personal experiences of Jesus' ministry, but he will share the coming glory with them and calls himself merely 'a fellow-elder'. That's a good example to set in a chapter calling on them to show humility.

5:2-4 There has never been a time when the leaders of God's people were not tempted to do things in the wrong way. For an Old Testament example see Numbers 20:1-12. The danger persists today, and Peter identifies some prime areas of particular concern.

5:5 The picture of humility as a garment fits very well with Peter's down-playing, in 3:3, of showy articles of clothing. Again, what we are like on the inside is shown to be much more important than outward appearance.

5:8 There is very little in the letter about demonic attack, and we neither can nor should build great theories about it on what Peter says here. Peter would acknowledge the spiritual realities which underlie the churches' suffering, but throughout the letter makes it clear that he wants the Christians to concentrate on responding correctly in the human arena. Notably, he focuses on perseverance and godly living, not on displays of dramatic spiritual power.

5:10 Promises that God will restore us are founded on a reminder of his character. He is 'the God of all grace', giving freely everything that his people need. He is also the one who calls us, and who will make sure that his call is effective (see 1 Thessalonians 5:23-24).

5:13 'Babylon' is used as a code word for Rome in both Jewish and Christian writings, drawing on traditions of wickedness and persecution linked to the older city. 'She who is in Babylon' refers to the church in Rome. 'Mark' is John Mark, who travelled with Paul and worked with him in Rome, where presumably he also grew closely involved with Peter's ministry.

5:14 The kiss was a custom in the churches, reflecting the Christians' brother-sister (not erotic!) relationships. It may have taken place at a specific point in a church service after Peter's letter was read out, or it may just have been done as the normal greeting and reminder of their closeness. The letter ends as it began (in 1:2) with a wish that its recipients would have peace. That must sometimes have seemed far away in their tough situation, but it was all the more necessary that they should be reminded that God could give them peace nonetheless.

YOUNG FOCUS

Adapt these starter ideas and questions according to the age of your children's or youth group, to give them a way into the passage.

There's a lot about humility in this passage. Spend a few minutes with the members telling each other, 'You're better than me because…'. That's easy enough and can be done without a great deal of sincerity. Discuss what being humble really requires of us and feels like in practice.

Have some pictures of happy sheep and sad sheep. Write on them ideas (suggested by group members) for what sort of shepherd would produce that reaction in a sheep – kind, bullying, gentle, generous, greedy and so on. List together the characteristics which members want to see in schoolteachers, group leaders and others in authority. Use 5:2-3 as a starting point or as a helpful checklist for the group's ideas.

Play a game which requires people to be alert: grandmother's footsteps, snap, Simon says or something similar. Then read 5:8. We need to stay alert!

Why is the devil compared to a lion here? What characteristics do they share? If the members met a lion, how would they try to avoid being eaten? Any clues here for resisting the devil? In the end, we can't do it on our own, but there are ways in which we can help ourselves.

Together, illustrate 5:10 with pictures from a magazine. Try to get the main concepts – grace (the hardest one), glory, suffering, restoration and strength. If you have lots of magazines, you could split the group into twos or threes and have a competition for the best set of pictures.

Because... Because...

1 PETER 5

GROUP SHEET

AIM
To have humility for the present and outrageous ambitions for the future

WAY IN
Have a silent discussion on the qualities of a Christian leader. Photocopy and cut out the slips on page 39, and distribute them to the group. Nominate one end of a table as 'Most important for a Christian leader' and the other as 'Least important'. Then, in silence, the group members take it in turns to place their slips wherever on that scale they think they should go. When all the slips are down, take it in turns (still in silence) to move slips which other people have put down. Keep this going for a while. See if you can come to a broad consensus about what is most and least important, or if some of the 'qualities' are really hard to decide about. Declare the silence finished, and talk through what people felt about the different issues raised. Were any vital qualities missing from the slips?

BIBLE STUDY Read 1 Peter 5
Looking at the text
Peter bases his appeal to the elders (5:1) in the present, the past and the future. How would his appeal lose some of its force if he missed out one of these perspectives?

What characteristics of Christian leadership does Peter focus on here?

What specific things does the chapter tell us about God?

What reasons does the chapter give us for taking care to have the right attitudes?

Applying the text
What other temptations are there for church leaders to avoid these days in addition to those mentioned by Peter? Are there any common problems which church members should be careful to avoid?

In practical terms, what does it mean for us to 'clothe ourselves with humility towards one another'?

How would you answer someone who said that 5:6,10 were just offering 'pie in the sky'?

How would we protect ourselves against being attacked by a lion? How can we protect ourselves against being attacked by the devil?

ACTION
Devise a mime, design a banner, write a song or poem, or do some other creative thing covering the main themes you have found in 1 Peter. Try to find an occasion to show or perform it in a church service.

ADDITIONAL QUESTIONS

1. How can we best support our church leaders? And how can we, in loving and constructive ways, keep them accountable to their flock?

2. What other images of Satan/the devil have you come across? Are they from the Bible? What is helpful about Peter's comparison of the devil with a lion?

3. Can you come up with a summary of 'the true grace of God', which Peter says is the subject of his letter (5:12)?

4. In the light of what he has said in this letter, why might Peter need to tell people, who presumably met together regularly, to greet one another with a kiss of love?

LEARNING ACTIVITIES

1. Better than you thought
Go round the group, with each person naming an everyday object which is thought of as lowly or not worth very much – a toilet, a dishcloth and so on. Then the group must think of at least three things which are good about each object. There is a link here (honestly!) with 5:6. How do we think of ourselves, and how does God think of us?

2. Better than ever
Use Lego, or similar construction play material, to create a tower, city or similar object. Once the group has suitably admired it, break it up. As a group, make something even better. Go on, go for it! Then read 5:10 again – this is what God promises to do for us if the pressures of Christian living get too much for us.

WORSHIP AND PRAYER

Verse 7 calls us to cast all our anxiety on our caring God. Share or write down the anxieties you have about the present and the future, and have a time of acknowledging them to God and asking him to give you peace about them. Note that our problems don't go away when we do this, but they come into the right perspective.

On a large piece of paper, each group member should draw (to the best of his or her ability!) an image of power – a bulging biceps muscle, a bolt of lightning and so on. It doesn't matter if some images are the same, or if they're a bit hard to recognize. Write GOD in big letters over all the images and, in the light of 5:11, praise him for his power. It may be good to include a time of sharing experiences of God working powerfully.

Read Psalm 126 together (or have one group member read it to you). This psalm links beautifully with Peter's theme of present suffering being replaced by joy through God's gracious love.

6 Getting it Straight

2 PETER 1

AIM
To appreciate that our faith is securely based, but never static

INTRODUCTION
This letter is concerned with showing up false teaching about the Christian message. In particular, there were teachers around who said that the second coming was not going to happen and that therefore there would be no judgement. If you believe that, it opens the way for all kinds of immoral behaviour.

Peter starts with a brief statement of the authentic Christian message and then, at the end of chapter 1, answers the objection that it is all a human invention. His language shows that he is writing to a church which has both Jewish and Greek influences; hence he uses some phrases which look rather strange to us. Imagine how carefully you would have to write if you were writing a letter to a group of readers which included some top lawyers, some rap artists and some people whose first language is different from yours.

NOTES

1:3 Peter stresses from the outset that God's grace is all we need for salvation and for godly living. The next verse shows that this is given through his promises – his word revealed in Scripture.

1:4 At face value this verse seems to imply that we can become 'part of' God. More likely Peter is referring to the 'god-like' gift of immortality to those who believe in him (compare John 5:24), or he may mean something like Paul's description of us as being 'in Christ' (Romans 8:1 and elsewhere). This is an example of Peter looking for ways of talking which would be meaningful to his Greek-influenced readers – we have to work a bit harder to understand than they would have had to!

1:5-9 Peter says that this list of Christian 'virtues' is what's needed for a fully productive life. If we neither possess nor value them, 1:9 raises the possibility that we may actually be fooling ourselves about having faith (the virtue from which the rest follow) at all.

1:10 God does all the work of bringing Christians to salvation, but it is necessary for us to live in the right way having been called. If there is no change in us and no true Christian walk, how can we say that we are trusting God?

1:12-15 Peter's prime concern is to ensure that his readers continue to remember and live by the teaching of the apostles. This has been what has given the Church its identity throughout the last twenty centuries, and is still what is crucial for us in holding firm to true faith.

1:16-18 Peter reminds his readers of the episode of the transfiguration: see for example Matthew 17:1-5. His point is that the message about Jesus is based in historical fact, and that God spoke up to emphasize its importance. It's not a human invention.

1:19-21 As in 1 Peter, a high view of the Old Testament is shown here. Its prophecies of Jesus, given by God and now interpreted through the New Testament, will remain vital for Christians until God's revelation is fully opened up in the heart of every believer at Jesus' second coming.

YOUNG FOCUS

Adapt these starter ideas and questions according to the age of your children's or youth group, to give them a way into the passage.

Discuss what is the most valuable thing that group members own (if you didn't do this in session 1). For Peter, it was probably his faith (1:1). Discuss why that was, and whether it's anywhere near true for any of the members (or leaders). If so, does that mean we could happily give up all our material possessions?

Verse 4 speaks very highly of God's promises. Point this out and make a number of promises about things that will happen during the session. (Don't be too honest about them – some need not happen, and we'll absolve you from your lies.) Ask the members to vote on which are likely to happen and which aren't serious. Look together at 2 Corinthians 1:20. All God's promises can be trusted. That's good news with regard to some important ones we'll come across later in 2 Peter.

Play chain tag, make daisy chains, tie everyone together in a long line, or do something else which conveys the idea of one thing leading to another. If you have time, equipment and appetite make a lot of pastry links and bake them into chains, then let two people start at opposite ends of each and eat their way to the middle. What's it all about? Verses 5 to 7: we all need to move on from quality to quality as we follow God's way.

Create a poster which pushes the ways in which Christians are effective and productive on God's behalf. Then measure yourselves against the standards you have set in it.

Talk about ways in which we can give a rich welcome to people who come to see us, particularly for something like a party. Have a party and try them out. But remember that the greatest party will be God's, and we're the ones seeking his rich welcome.

See who can come up with the best slogan beginning, 'The Bible is like light because…'. Have a fabulous prize – perhaps you could present it at the party you've just planned. More importantly, take a fridge to your meeting and ask why the Bible is like a fridge. The answer is not because it's cold or it contains tons of good things (although it does), but because the light in it has no effect unless you open it. Cunning and also rather challenging, huh?

GROUP SHEET

Getting it Straight

2 PETER 1

AIM
To appreciate that our faith is securely based, but never static

WAY IN
What objections do friends, workmates and so on raise against Christianity today? Discuss how you would answer the charge that 'It's all just made up'.

BIBLE STUDY Read 2 Peter 1

Looking at the text
In what ways might early Christians have been tempted to 'put Peter on a pedestal' (1:1-3)? How does he attempt in these verses to prevent them from doing this?

God's promises are 'very great and precious'. What specific promises do you know from the Bible? Share particularly precious ones with each other.

Compare 1:5-7 with Galatians 5:22-23 (a better known list of 'virtues'). What do the lists have in common and what does Peter add here? Does it matter that the lists are different?

Peter acknowledges that his readers already know the things he is telling them. So why does he bother to do so?

In what is Peter putting his confidence, according to 1:16-21?

What are the day and star referred to in 1:19?

Applying the text
Can you think of any times in the past week when you particularly had to draw on any of the qualities listed in 1:5-7?

How might we be able to assess whether we are making progress along the lines that Peter urges in 1:5-7? (Note that 1:8 says we should have these qualities 'in increasing measure'.)

Verse 15 shows that Peter was determined to pass on the truth to those who came after him. What things about God are you particularly keen to make sure that the next generation know? How are you going about making sure of it?

What means can we or should we use to make sure that we 'pay attention' to the words of the prophets?

ACTION
Produce a banner or other visual device illustrating the virtues in 1:5-7 as links in a chain, steps in a staircase or something similar. Have it displayed somewhere prominent to remind you of the qualities we should constantly be developing as Christians.

ADDITIONAL QUESTIONS

1. How would you answer someone who said that the qualities listed in 1:5-7 are old-fashioned and unnecessary nowadays?

2. How can we go about 'refreshing each other's memories' about the basics of the Christian life, as Peter seeks to do for his readers? It may not be by writing letters, but what practical help can we give each other in this?

3. Have you come across any 'cleverly invented stories' about Jesus, put about by cults, popular books or television, or anywhere else? How do know what is true about Jesus and what is just a story?

LEARNING ACTIVITIES

1. Sanctification Street
Video in advance some short scenes from TV soaps which involve conflict between the characters. After watching each, discuss what difference it might have made to the situation if one or more of the characters had shown one of the virtues from those listed in 1:5-7.

2. Spud-U-Love
Get a potato (preferably a bit scruffy, muddy and knobbly) and transfigure it (with whatever clothes, jewellery and so on you like) into the most beautiful potato on earth. Keep it on permanent display (until the smell gets too bad) as a (somewhat oblique) reminder of the wonderful transfiguration of the historical Jesus. If you're heavily into potatoes, use several and have a competition. But remember, God does it best!

WORSHIP AND PRAYER

Black out the room and give everyone a candle or a torch. Having read 1:19, pray prayers of thanks to God for his word. As people pray, they should light their candle, switch on their torch etc. Prayers might be as simple as 'Thank you for [the name of a Bible book]'. Some people might read out a favourite short passage and leave time for everyone to think about it. Aim to have a really bright room by the end of this time.

Verses 12 to 15 show the gospel being passed on from person to person, like the links in a chain. Provide everyone with a copy of the Apostles' Creed (*The Alternative Service Book*, page 80) and link your arms in a circle. Someone reads the first phrase of the Creed, then their neighbour reads the next, and so on. Try to read it as it should be: not a series of dry statements, but a declaration of praise.

We don't have any photos of the transfiguration, so ask people beforehand to bring their own photos of striking 'nature' scenes. Ideally these would include mountains, but it doesn't matter if not and it's OK if they're cut out of magazines. Look at the photos together and hear any personal stories attached to them. Then thank God for the beauty in them and for the far greater beauty and importance of his Son.

Danger Ahead!

2 PETER 2

AIM
To be aware of the dangers posed by false teaching, and to be ready to confront them

INTRODUCTION
There are serious dangers for the church in what Peter outlines here. However, just as great in the long run is the danger for those who lead Christians astray. False teachers may seem to have everything going for them in the short term, but in the end God's triumph, and their disaster, is certain. That long-term perspective, however, doesn't reduce the need to fight falsehood here and now. You may find that some people need to air (and rethink) their attitudes to what is truth, in the light of Peter's tough talking in this chapter.

NOTES

2:1 There is a desperate need for Christians to know and declare the truth and to denounce untruth. At the same time, of course, we must remember to love our enemies (Matthew 5:44) and seek to win them for the truth.

2:4 The angels referred to are the 'sons of God' we hear of in Genesis 6:1-4. Their rebelliousness and lustfulness led to punishment. Peter's point here is that if God has the power to deal with angelic beings, then he can certainly carry out his judgements on humans.

2:5-7 The story of Noah can be found in Genesis 6, and that of Lot's escape from Sodom and Gomorrah in Genesis 19. Again, Peter sees the Christian message illustrated through the Old Testament as well as through Jesus and the early church: judgement on the wicked and delivery of the righteous has happened before and will happen again, definitively, at the second coming.

2:10 The false teachers were sceptical about the second coming with its judgement of evil powers, and perhaps therefore about the very existence of such powers. They therefore took a stupidly arrogant attitude towards the devil and his forces.

2:15-16 For the story of Balaam and his donkey, see Numbers 22.

2:17 The picture here is of things apparently full of the promise of life-giving water, which turn out to be utterly unable to deliver. There could be no greater contrast with God's promises, which are always fulfilled.

2:19 The freedom that the false teachers were promising was freedom from judgement: if there was to be no second coming, God wouldn't be judging anyone. Therefore they claimed that there was no need to live by any kind of moral rules.

2:20-21 We sometimes have trouble with the thought that people may be able to know something of Jesus and then fall away, but the picture here is quite in harmony with Jesus' image of the seed that fell on the rocky places or among thorns (see Matthew 13 for the parable of the sower). Receiving the word is how we know Jesus. It gives added urgency to Peter's appeal in 1:10.

2:22 Peter's disdainful dismissal of the false teachers underlines the importance of the truth, and the vileness of what such teachers represent.

YOUNG FOCUS

Adapt these starter ideas and questions according to the age of your children's or youth group, to give them a way into the passage.

Provide a basin of water and a towel, and a beach ball. One leader is allowed to throw the ball at the group members. Anyone who is hit must shout 'Yuk!' very loudly and wash their hands before continuing. Keep it frantic. Afterwards, talk about what it would have been like if you had used mud, paint or something similar instead of the ball. Move on to the need to avoid what is wrong – it's very hard to wash away if it gets hold of us.

Share examples of lies that have been uncovered in the news or the soaps, and how destructive their effects can be. The truth about Jesus is vital, and can be found in the Bible (as we saw in the last session).

If you want a roughish game, get one member to try to rescue another who is inside a circle made up of all the other members. Those in the circle can only offer passive resistance, but they will normally prevent the rescue. Or play some kind of wide game which involves rescuing tennis balls from another team's camp. The point is, God is brilliant at this stuff (2:9). Get the survivors to praise him for that!

Based on 2:2, play follow my leader, causing havoc and trashing the room. Survey the ruins. Then play again, putting things back. Draw the parallels with people following bad ways and God stepping in to put things right.

After a hot and exhausting game, hand round some empty glasses or cans and invite people to have a refreshing drink. Or offer to cool them down with a fan and use a blow heater instead. That's the lesson of 2:17 – false teachers and leaders have exactly that effect, and worse. Now take pity on the members. Give them cool drinks, wash their feet and encourage them to thank God for what they feel.

When you reach 2:22, wash a pig and watch what it does next. Or, if you have a dog, … oh, no …

GROUP SHEET

Danger Ahead!

2 PETER 2

AIM
To be aware of the dangers posed by false teaching, and to be ready to confront them

WAY IN
Each group member has to say three things about himself or herself. Two must be true and one false. The rest of the group has to try to guess which is the false item. Be devious: you don't often get a chance to lie to the rest of the group, do you?

BIBLE STUDY Read 2 Peter 2

Looking at the text
Compare 2:3 with 1 Peter 5:2. What was a basic temptation for these false teachers? Check that out with Colossians 3:5.

What other indications should warn us if someone allegedly proclaiming Jesus is not in fact doing so? (2:13-14)

What facts about the false teachers is Peter trying to convey in 2:17-18? Compare these verses with the utterly different picture painted in John 4:13-14.

Why do you think Peter says that it would have been better for the false teachers never to have known anything of Jesus (2:20-21)?

Applying the text
Is it possible to be *too* concerned today with looking for false teaching?

Is it worse for a Christian leader to lie than for anyone else to do so?

Lot's attitude, recounted in 2:7-8, reflects the call of the psalmist in Psalm 97:10. How can we show in practice that we hate evil, without merely seeming 'holier-than-thou' to those around us?

Do we truly live as if the second coming is a reality? Are we in any danger of paying lip service to it while living a lifestyle which suggests to those around us that we don't really believe in it?

ACTION
Find out about the beliefs and activities of any pseudo-Christian cults which operate in your area. Be sure that you know the biblical grounds for refuting them, and keep an active look-out for opportunities to tell people the true position.

ADDITIONAL QUESTIONS

1. Peter frequently illustrates his points from the Old Testament. How well do we know that part of the Bible? Do we know the various ways it functions in helping us understand our faith?

2. In the light of 2 Peter 1:19-21 and 2:1-2, how can we tell true messages from God from false ones?

3. Which do you think are more dangerous, head-on attacks on Christianity or distorted versions of it?

LEARNING ACTIVITIES

1. Defend the faith
Hand out some slips of paper with modern heresies written on them – think of your own or photocopy the ones on page 40. Each group member should try to spend one minute speaking against the heresy they have been given. Other members are allowed to help out if necessary. It's important that we know how to argue against the lies that are in circulation – look again at 1 Peter 3:15-16 for further instructions.

2. Get out of town
Design a 'Wanted' poster, featuring a false teacher with all the faults mentioned by Peter in this chapter. Finish with the phrase 'Not wanted by anybody here, but wanted by God for final judgement'. Keep it as a reminder of what to avoid.

3. Same old trouble
Find out about some of the major heresies which have caused trouble in the Church over the centuries. Do any of them seem familiar? The chances are that the same old lies are still in circulation somewhere today. Roll on, the second coming!

WORSHIP AND PRAYER

Take time to reflect on 2:8. What distresses us now, in society and in the Church? Pray about it, not forgetting to repent about any part we ourselves play in what is wrong.

Find a copy of one of the great creeds of the Church: the Apostles' (which we used in the last session) or Nicene versions are probably best, although if you have a group full of Mensa members you could try the Athanasian one. Say it, loud and clear, together and then pray prayers of thanks and praise based on the various truths it affirms about God. That should keep you going for a week or so, and it's a great way to protect ourselves against false teaching. Look in *The Alternative Service Book* for the Apostles' Creed (page 80) and the Nicene Creed (page 123). St Athanasius' Creed may be tracked down in the *Book of Common Prayer*.

Much of this chapter is negative in tone. Identify the main points Peter makes and think, 'What's the other side of the coin?' In other words, take the opposite of the negative things Peter draws our attention to, and give thanks for that: good, biblical teaching; godly living by Christian leaders, and so on.

8

Future Perfect!

2 PETER 3

AIM
To sum up Peter's message and to set a course for the future.

INTRODUCTION
This chapter rounds off the whole Petrine corpus. Good phrase, huh? OK, it finishes off Peter's letters. It does so by going over some of the same, familiar ground again (because it's so important) and adding a 'So what?' If God's going to do what he has said, what should Peter's readers do about it? The answer is pretty clear, and it applies to us as well. So let's do it.

NOTES

3:1-2 This is Peter's declared purpose in writing to the churches. Note again the insistence on the reliability of the Old Testament and of the apostolic teaching.

3:3 The 'last days' are the whole time between Jesus' earthly ministry and his second coming: there is no reference to a narrow band of time either at the time of Peter or immediately before the second coming.

3:6 One of Peter's favourite anecdotes makes its last appearance – another reference to the flood of Noah's time, which proved God's ability to carry out judgement. No one who has read these letters can say they weren't warned that judgement is firmly on God's agenda.

3:8-9 Our obsession with diaries and calendars is pretty immaterial to God. His plans are on course. With so much stress on the context of judgement in this letter, it's important to keep clearly in our minds this declaration of God's patience and loving purposes for humanity. The prospect of rescue from the coming wrath (see 1 Thessalonians 1:10) is constantly on offer as long as he allows human history to continue.

3:11 In session 1 we heard a call to be holy, just as God is holy (1 Peter 1:15-16). The same point is made here. There is no room for slacking when it comes to living a life that pleases God.

3:12 If God is so firmly in charge, how can we possibly speed the coming of the day of judgement? Simply, by repenting, leading others to repentance, and leading godly lives together. Then his patience (3:9) need not continue.

3:16 Note that Paul's writings here are given the same rank as 'the other Scriptures': that is, the Old Testament. We can see the New Testament, as we know it, beginning to take shape. It's comforting to know that Paul's writings, which make up such a large part of it, were already held in such esteem – even if some things in them are 'hard to understand', which seems a bit like the pot calling the kettle black.

3:18 In this last verse, where we might expect a phrase such as 'Glory to God', we have instead an offering of glory to Jesus. There was a similar surprise in 2 Peter 1:1. The realization that Jesus is in fact God is firmly implied.

YOUNG FOCUS

Adapt these starter ideas and questions according to the age of your children's or youth group, to give them a way into the passage.

Ask the group to pick out from the chapter the things that Peter thinks are most important. Do they match what we focus on in our daily thinking?

Share what it feels like to wait for something you're really looking forward to. Are there any times when members have had to wait a long time but it's been really worth it when the event has finally happened?

Time seems to move slowly when we're impatient. Ask people to shut their eyes while you time a minute going by. When they think a minute has gone, they should silently put up a hand. See who gets closest, and then look together at 3:8. Fortunately, God's sense of time is very good.

Gather suggestions for inappropriate things to do in the supermarket queue, dentist's waiting room, and so on. From 3:11,14,17-18, look together at the need to live right while waiting for Jesus' return.

Get everyone to bounce a ball against a wall, saying the name of a non-Christian friend each time. How many bounces can they manage before they lose concentration and drop the ball? Rejoice that God's patience and concentration are so great. Resolve together to keep praying for the friends they have been naming, mirroring the patience of God.

Draw or list the things that members would like to have in their dream homes. Heaven will be better (3:13). Discuss the things that people expect to be characteristic of heaven. God's preparing it for us even now. How prepared are we?

Bring in a selection of pot plants, vegetables, puppies and babies. Talk about what helps things to grow. Given Peter's concluding command to 'grow in the grace and knowledge' of Jesus, how can we make it easier for ourselves to grow, and how can we help each other?

Future Perfect!

2 PETER 3

AIM
To sum up Peter's message and to set a course for the future

WAY IN
Share together what each group member would do if they knew that they had one day left before the end of the world. What if it was one hour?

BIBLE STUDY Read 2 Peter 3
Looking at the text
What is the main objection that Peter expects people to raise to the message concerning the second coming of Jesus?

What is his answer to that objection?

The day of the Lord won't nick your car. How, then, will it be 'like a thief'?

In the light of the second coming, how should Christians behave, and why?

What are our safeguards against falling away from our faith?

If Peter were asked to put into one sentence the message of this chapter, how do you think he would express it?

Applying the text
For what reasons do we meet with and speak to our fellow Christians? Does anything need changing in the light of 3:1-2?

Is it realistic or desirable to make the theme of judgement a prominent part of our church's preaching and our own evangelism today?

How may 3:12-13 affect our approach to a) environmental issues and b) our possessions?

Are we 'looking forward' (3:14) to what Peter is foretelling? If not, why not? And what can we do about it?

Note how Peter addresses his readers in 3:1,8,14 and 17. What relationship do we expect between church leaders and 'ordinary' members today? Can we do more to draw close together?

ACTION
Think what evangelistic steps you can take to try to help people in your neighbourhood not to perish, but to come to repentance. And don't stop at thinking: do some planning now, so that the impetus provided by Peter's letter does not get lost.

ADDITIONAL QUESTIONS

1. There is plenty of 'fire' imagery here about the destruction of the world. The Bible does not make it clear whether there is a fiery hell or not. Does it make a difference to our evangelism?

2. The clear implication of 3:8-9 is that God is delaying establishing the fullness of his richly deserved and overwhelming glory, for the sake of sinners who have no claim on him. When did we last show a similar patience and other-centredness?

3. We don't live in a patient age. Does that make it harder to tell people why the second coming is taking so long to arrive?

4. What does it mean to 'grow in the grace and knowledge of our Lord and Saviour Jesus Christ'?

LEARNING ACTIVITIES

1. Wouldn't it be lovely?
In twos or threes, make a list of what you would like to see in your own 'earthly paradise'. Don't be too serious. Share your lists and then discuss what you expect to see in heaven. The reality will be even better!

2. Easy does it
Do something together that demands a lot of patience. Have a competition to see who can outstare everyone else without blinking. Or a slow bicycle race (that's especially good if you haven't ridden a bike for years – borrow some bikes – but don't blame us if you fall off). Be thankful that God's patience is greater than ours.

3. Two for the price of one
This is Peter's 'second letter'. What can you recall about the contents of the two letters? Share what has stuck in your mind from earlier sessions. If nothing has, you could try asking for your money back for this book. But don't hold your breath.

WORSHIP AND PRAYER

How patient did God have to be with us? Share your stories of coming to know God, and thank him for the many different ways he gets the news of his love for us into our thick skulls.

Read together Revelation 21:1-5. That's another view of what it will be like at the end of time. Reflect for a while in silence on what it will be like to have no more death, mourning, crying or pain. Pray as seems appropriate.

Agree to pray 3:18 for each other for some days or weeks to come, and remember to do it. What a great thing to know that someone is praying that you'll grow in Jesus' grace and knowledge!

Finally, worship God by living holy and godly lives as you look forward to the day of God and speed its coming! May God help us all to do that.

Because of Him...

This simple mime for a small group of people is based on 1 Peter 2:21-25. See the Worship and Prayer section of Session 2 (page 13). It may be accompanied by a reading of the passage or done in silence. Take it nice and slowly.

1 Peter 2:21-25

Verse 21
To this you were called, because Christ suffered for you, leaving you an example, that you should follow in his steps.

Central figure beckons people to come, then turns and walks slowly away, with others fitting into the same stride pattern.

Verse 22
'He committed no sin, and no deceit was found in his mouth.'

Central figure shows hands, then raises them as if to heaven; then indicates mouth and raises hands again. Others bow heads as if in reverence.

Verse 23
When they hurled their insults at him, he did not retaliate; when he suffered, he made no threats. Instead, he entrusted himself to him who judges justly.

The others change to an accusing crowd, with stabbing, pointing fingers, pushing central figure around. Central figure offers no resistance, but bows head, kneels and spreads arms, palms upwards. Accusers freeze, pointing, in horseshoe around central figure.

Verse 24
He himself bore our sins in his body on the tree, so that we might die to sins and live for righteousness; by his wounds you have been healed.

Central figure walks a little way apart, alone, and makes a crucifixion shape. Head should be thrown back to suggest pain, but don't be too melodramatic. After a short while, the accusers kneel. The central figure comes to them, raises them to their feet, encircles them with arms (as far as is practicable, depending on how many of them there are).

Verse 25
For you were like sheep going astray, but now you have returned to the Shepherd and Overseer of your souls.

Central figure walks slightly apart; then repeat the routine from verse 21.

Silent Discussion

Copy and cut out these words and phrases below to use with the discussion activity in Session 5 (page 24).

love	mind-reading ability
patience	a servant attitude
sense of humour	quick reader
preaching ability	hospitable
good singing voice	strict disciplinarian
humility	always cheerful
a peace-maker	own teeth and hair
sporting skills	disregard of money
administrative ability	speaking in tongues
fashion sense	attractive to the opposite sex
nice car	
holiday cottage in Wales	good memory for faces
excellent Bible knowledge	ability to enthuse people
commitment to prayer	knowledge of modern music

Defend the Faith

Welcome to 'Modern Heresy Corner'. Copy and cut out the following statements to use with the Learning Activity on page 33.

Jesus was just a good teacher.	All religions have the same message, so it doesn't matter which you follow.
We are all God – we just need to discover the divine within ourselves.	The Bible is a coded message from aliens, and we need to monitor radio signals from outer space in order to be saved.
God's great desire is that people should be happy.	
It doesn't matter what you believe, as long as you're sincere.	We can't trust the Bible now because we know so much more about science and how human beings work.
God is love, so he couldn't condemn anyone.	
We'll all get another chance to say yes to God, in another life.	As long as you live a good life, you'll go to heaven.